I LOVE ANGER
FOR TEENS

TRAINING WORKBOOK

Based on the bestselling book *"I Love Anger"*

Isaac Rowe

I LOVE ANGER

FOR TEENS

By Isaac Rowe

ISBN-13: 9781791903855

CONTENTS

DISCLAIMER

This workbook was developed to coach you with tools and tips for anger management. It will help you better understand and manage anger and the role it's taking in your life. It is important for you to recognize anger and its effect on your life and others lives. This book is to aid in your own personal development. I make no claim that you will be absolutely free of anger. However this workbook is a tool that can be used and this method may not be for everyone.

INSTRUCTIONS

Hello, I pray that this book I is a blessing to you and that you are ready for the next steps in your journey. I designed this workbook to be a training tool for youth who want to bring anger management into their everyday lives. I call it a "training workbook" because anything that you train in like exercising for example, requires a process, practice and discipline. The concepts in my book will help you manage anger. Using this training workbook you will understand anger and its effects on you. How can you effectively manage anger in a powerful way?

I wrote this book for those who want to discover who they are. I want you to take a walk in my shoes and see for yourself that in some ways you and I are the same. We all have asked ourselves "Why am I so upset about this issue?" and "Why can't I shake it?" I foresaw my life ending if I continued to allow anger to consume every aspect of my life. I had to change. Do you really and truthfully want a change?

This book is for the ones who feel they are depressed, suicidal, addicted, abused, rejected and unloved. I ask let us be real with ourselves today. Let our hearts and minds be open to new ideas and ways of thinking. I will be here every step of the way. You will read the following pages of the book of *I Love Anger* and then complete each session. I will take you on a journey of my life and hopefully you will see yourself and find a way your way to freedom.

Let's begin..

PRE ANGER SURVEY

Please answer the following questions as accurately and as completely as possible.

1. How many times do you get angry? (Check one that applies)
[ ] less than 5 times a day
[ ] more than 5 times a day.
[ ] several times a week.
[ ] a few times a month.
[ ] rarely.

2. I get angry when? (Check all that apply)
[ ] My friends are being bullied verbally, emotionally or physically.
[ ] I am treated unfairly.
[ ] I Feel depressed.
[ ] Name-calling or teasing/bullied
[ ] People will not listen to me. (Friends, Parents, Teachers, Other_____)
[ ] Someone tries to take something from me
[ ] People don't give me a chance.
[ ] People reject me or don't accept me
[ ] I am not loved by family
[ ] I'm not able to voice my opinion
[ ] Someone damages my property
[ ] Anyone pushes or hits me, or someone close to me
[ ] People don't understand my feelings
[ ] People don't have time for me.
[ ] I feel like I don't matter.
[ ] People tell me what to do
[ ] Losing a game or a contest
[ ] Mistreatment of animals

3. When I get angry I? (Check all that apply)
[ ] Hit someone or something.
[ ] Hurt myself
[ ] Throw things
[ ] I tell a friend teacher or parent.
[ ] Keep it inside
[ ] I raise my voice and get really loud
[ ] Become cynical or sarcastic.
[ ] Relax and Breathe
[ ] Use anger management tools
[ ] Think about how I can get even.
[ ] Smile and play it off as a joke.
[ ] I argue and curse at people
[ ] Blackout
Other _____

INTRODUCTION

"Ever feel angry? Gut-wrenching, fist-pounding, can't-shake-it-off, straight up volatile? Do you look at the world with a bent brow, ready to pick a fight? Does anger make you feel sick, anxious, powerful, or validated? Does it control your life? Good! That means you picked up the right book. The following pages will take you on a roller coaster of mind-changing and thought-provoking experiences that will teach you to understand, challenge, and control your emotional responses. It will help heal your relationship with your parents, teachers, your parents, your friends and yourself. You will come to learn the PURPOSE of anger in your life, as well as the role it's played in mine, so that you may live a life of freedom and peace.

Understanding and managing my own anger has been the greatest struggle and triumph in my life. By sharing my extreme highs and lows with this infectious emotion, you will encounter the reasons I used anger as both a shield and weapon, to "protect" me from a tough upbringing. You'll witness my anger towards everyone and see how my life transformed over the years, from a life of fear and shame to one of personal power. As you probably know, the journey is rough, but not impossible. It is my intention that you take my lessons, insight, and understanding of anger to apply them to your own life. Caution: I don't hold back.

My story starts with my parents coming from two very different backgrounds. My father is from Georgia, where his family raised hogs and owned pecan orchards. My mother, from Texas, comes from a very religious background. I don't know where my anger began. I did not come out of the womb angry, but growing up, it's what I learned to be. I hated—well, hate is a big word—I was dissatisfied with all people, including myself. Around the age of 9 my life took some turns because of my parent's choices.

My parents met in college. I would say their relationship started out pretty good, normal. Life seemed as normal as the sky was blue.

While my parents were working during the day, I spent a lot of time at my papal (my grandfather) and grandma's house. Their home was out in the country on some land by the lake. My papal taught me many skills from sports and fishing, to working with my hands. He took me on rides in his truck. He let me drive sitting in his lap as I steered, staying in between the dirt road lanes. Texas boys learn how to drive early and I was good. I only wrecked once into a fence! He showed me how to shoot my first hunting rifle. Our hunts consisted of him going to sleep, and me waking him up when I could see the deer. When I woke him, he made so much noise that the deer would always run away. This was before Gameboys and all those fancy gadgets that kept kids occupied. I thought the rifle was going to take my arm off because of the kick back. I had a bruise on my arm for a week. I also remember papal showing me how to play baseball. I was on the local little league team and apparently, I really sucked. I wanted to play because a lot of my friends at school were playing. My team was called the A's and I was the alternate of the substitutes at the end of the roster. As my grandfather took time out of his busy schedule to enhance my baseball skills, I worked even harder in my spare time. One day at a game, my mother attended and asked the coach to give me a chance to prove myself. Honestly, I think they got tired of watching the other kids play. My time came towards the end of the season, and that day, I was at bat. "Crack!" I got a double, which means I made it to second base. The second time around, I got another double. The third time around, I hit a triple! In the outfield, I played center field. On a big game play, I threw the ball from the gate to home plate and stopped the opposing team from getting a homerun. I never knew I could throw that far; I shocked myself. After that, my coach then turned around and said to my mother "He's coming along, ain't he?" My mother cut her eyes as she looked at him and smiled at him in silence, as if she always knew. It's amazing to me how one person can change or affect another person's life. It is important to realize the effect each and every one of us has on one another. With just that small comment, and my mother's affirmation, I felt glorious. Papal was a pastor of a church where he pastored for many years until his death, by a car accident. This was, and is still, the most hurtful thing I deal with on a daily basis.

I was a young man, discovering myself and it was confusing trying to figure out life. My papal was my center in life. He taught me so much and all of a sudden, he was gone. I finally understood what happened and realized that everyone will die one day. We all have an expiration date for our time on earth. In a way I was mad, but also felt blessed. Yes, I was a little selfish because I still needed time for him to show me things. I wasn't ready for him to go just yet. I always thought he would live forever. I like to believe my grandfather's spirit still lives inside of me.

Note: I am the oldest grandson so I spent a lot of time with my grandfather. The man and role model in my life was no longer here. My father was not a bad father at this time; I just did not learn that much from him, he was still discovering himself. His father passed when he was in college, so he was just out there living life. He was a provider of security but he did not spend much time or hand down information to me in the area of becoming a man. Most things I learned from grandfather, as well as other men, movies, and TV. No one walked me through the process of becoming a man. I currently mentor men with life struggles. Most of them are fatherless or never had a good relationship with their father. I want you to know that no matter what circumstances you acquire in life, it is never too late to restore any relationship you may have. You still have the opportunity make things right.

Well, my family and I moved to central, Texas, along with some friends of my parents, to start a new life. There was new scenery and a new environment. The city was very busy compared to where we came from, where everyone knew pretty much everyone. These friends of my parents got hooked on drugs. This was the trend back in the day. They were grown, so I cannot blame their friends for their participation, only the exposure. That's a real friend, huh? They got hooked and made it their god.

Moving had its fair share of interesting situations for me. For starters, I was hit by a truck which jumped the curb while I was riding my bicycle. Who hits a 10-year-old kid on his bike and leaves him on the ground? Did he care whether or not I was hurt or dead? Did he have dreams of me screaming, that make it hard for him to sleep? Who knows. These are hopes I had for him, as my anger boiled and boiled. I wanted him to suffer, like I was.

So, after this, I was finally making some friends, before some REAL stuff went down. One of my friends ran into a car coming down a hill pretty fast. The car's brakes went out and the driver was unable to stop. He crashed into the car, flipped over atop the car, cracked his skull on the hot Texas street, which caused his brain to come out of his skull. I'll never forget it. My friend became a vegetable; he had no response to anything. No more video games for us. No more running down the street, chasing each other. The people around me were no stranger to tragedies such as this; I'd seen young people who'd witnessed their parents murdered or people dead on the street. We may have different walks of life, but if you are like me, after too many encounters of people dying too young and too fast, my sensitivity of death became kind of numb. It was a distant feeling, an unreal experience, just knowing that one day, my day would come. All I could do is stare, disappear into "Isaac's world" in my mind, where I didn't want to believe this stuff was a part of my life. I needed to put whatever feeling this was away until I could understand it. You're probably thinking, "Dang, all of this happened back to back?" Well, what I can remember are the scars of my memory. I only felt and anticipated more pain. I waited until it came versus trying to live my life. I stacked anger, hurt, pain and disappointment on top of one another because I didn't have the tools to be able to cope with what I was feeling. It grew day after day after day, like a volcano waiting for time to shine. This eruption was the main guest at my pity parties. I wasted years throwing them for myself, hosting the anger, blaming myself and others for things I could not control. Even though I don't experience "pity parties" for myself anymore, they were necessary to realize that I was stuck and needed a way out!

My parents did okay in life. Things were good, I believe, until some things started to happen like drinking, smoking and drugs. My parents did the drugs together. I guess to say they did it together is a plus huh? An example of unity? Well, the drug addiction really began to set in comfortably when we started stealing shoes from stores. Yes, this is illegal and you probably have heard of this before. We walked in, put our old shoes in the box, and walked out with the new shoes on our feet. Hey! New shoes on my feet! I always felt uncomfortable, like I wasn't supposed to be doing this, but I trusted my mom that this was ok. She would say, "go ahead, walk to the car, and don't look back, Isaac." She later came out. She would get my brother and me new shoes this way. "Why did we do this?" I asked myself. "Isn't this stealing because we didn't pay for it?" I believed that it was right to steal if you really needed it. So one day, my brother, a friend and I went on the bus to go to local mall to steal some clothes. Our friend needed some new shoes because his shoes were torn up and talking at the end with the little flap, you know. We did what mama had taught us: Try the shoes on and put yours back in the box. We were successful, so we decided to try it at a department store and unfortunately the sales lady didn't think our method was so sly: we got caught. Rule number one when stealing: never take an amateur to steal with you, I guess we were all amateurs in that respect. They caught us in so many camera angles stealing in the store. They caught us as we walked out of the store. They were waiting on us at the door because it's not stealing until you exit the store with the merchandise. The guy grabbed us and took us into a back room full of cameras. The streets of the eastside began to make its way inside my speech. I'm like "Whoa!" If I had known this, I would never have stolen. The security called our parents and my father left work to get us. We got a whipping from him and from my mom. My dad had never whipped us before. I believe that is the only time he actually whipped us. Most of the time, it was what he called a jack slap or a back hand lick. Our friend's mom, who was with us when we stole, came and she made him take his shoes back. I told her they weren't from this store; we stole them from another store. It's funny how I was trying to justify. We didn't steal the shoes from them and that was okay because we didn't get caught. We were home free. Besides, he really needed the shoes more than we did. As a mother, she should have bought him some shoes and socks, instead of letting him walk around with flapping shoes. I do not know if you ever have worn talking shoes, where the front top part and the bottom separated to the point where you can see the toes. I know how embarrassing it is to walk around school like that. You feel like you are nothing. All the other kids laughed at him and we were laughed at too, because we hung together. Have you ever had kids make fun of you? Or are you the one who picks on other kids? Well to let you know I developed a certain complex about myself; a feeling that you I helpless. Nobody wants to hang with you because they might get that "poverty disease" too. You could do a quick fix with super glue but it doesn't hold for very long. You have to be very careful walking because you don't want it to come loose. In high school, I had some black and red popular 90's basketball sneakers. They got so bad from wearing them that the bottom gel-like center of the heel came out and my feet were exposed. To stop it from getting my socks wet and falling through the hole with the heel of my foot, I had to rig it with some cut pieces of that good wire hanger(not that cheap weak stuff nowadays), and a plastic grocery bag. I had to put the hanger pieces across the hole to reinforce it and put another insole from another shoe to hold the bag down. I had to do that just about every week. Not everyone gets new shoes every year for school, but we got a new pair every couple of years. What's crazy is, even when I had turned 16 and got a job I still didn't think I deserved nice things. This is a prime example of the poverty mentality. Nobody wants to be poor. Children can't help who they live with and where. We could change our world if we would change the way we look at our situation. Just because you lived in the projects, and your relatives lived there before you, does not mean you have to continue this in your generation. Move somewhere else! Get out the hood! I see young babies that didn't know anything about anything grow up to become criminals, now dead or in prison. This cycle has to stop somewhere. Poverty is a mindset that is conditioned over time. The "hood" groomed the children to be thugs and criminals. This could happen because of the angry people in the hood. They do not want anything in life, so they tell you "sorry, this is it when it's not. This is their reality and they are forcing that onto others, like me and you.

Somehow times changed as my parents struggled and as a result, we ended up at a mission for the homeless. We stayed at a community mission for what seemed to be a lifetime. We lived in a one-room efficiency apartment.

Children suffer because of their parents and guardians; the ones that should be trusted are not responsible. The mission was not a good place to be. There were roaches and trash everywhere. It was not ideal for any family, even a poor one. As a kid, I didn't even understand how poor we were until one of my teachers asked me for my address and I couldn't tell them. I said, "At the mission up the street." They were like, "Um, okay..." Since then, they automatically treated me as if I was poor and beneath them, and so did the other students. I received a different attitude from them and I always felt as though I was a special case. I was treated like I didn't belong there.

The kids didn't want to be around me. None of the kids would play with me during recess. I was mad at my teachers and my parents for making me feel this way. I did not believe I should have to feel this. I felt so ashamed that I was poor. I thought to myself, "Is poverty normal?" The kids at school treated me differently because the teacher treated me like a "case". Good thing she wasn't a real case worker, or she'd be out of a job! By the way, remember when I mentioned earlier that my mom, brother and I were in the mission and she was pregnant?

My father battled cancer at a tender age. Back then, it was considered uncommon. He had a severe case and when they found out, they rushed him to the operating room because he was on the verge of dying. The doctors gave him a 50/50 chance to live after surgery and chemotherapy. The doctor had asked him, "Do you have any means of living?" He said, "My kids."

Growing up, life was extremely challenging for us. It was difficult for my parents to agree on anything. Meanwhile their drug of choice was tearing us apart. They eventually split up again and went their separate ways. We decided to go back to west Texas where we found housing. Finally, some sense of stability was found in the place where so many memories began. I was in the sixth grade by now and discovered an uncanny gift for percussion. I was finally able, after waiting for so long, to join and play in the band. The landlord's son had an old drum with a case that my mother bought for me. It was a blessing until she pawned it for drugs. I have to look on the bright side and say that at least my grandfather gave me my first pair of drumsticks. I guess he grew tired of me beating on the walls. I was so excited! The bottom of the drum case was broken, so that when I walked, it would fall out. I attempted to fix it with some duct tape, but it wasn't a permanent fix and it would still fall out. I grew a bit popular, only because I knew how to play the song "Wipeout" really fast by The Surfaris. I would set up every morning and I had a crowd around me and others wanted to play too. I started at the 8th chair and ended up around 3rd or 4th chair usually. I always got beat on technical things.

Meanwhile, my mother became involved in an abusive relationship with a guy who also had a drug habit. His drug of choice can do a lot of damage mentally and physically. After they would go partying, they would argue and fight. Until one day, the beating was no longer one-sided. We were so afraid for our lives; we beat him with a pellet gun, a crescent wrench, and a bat. I was young, but I was proud that we could protect my mother. The aggression and anger I had behind it was sweet. It seemed a little wicked that I would think in this way at such a young age. As you can see, this was quite a bit for an 11-year-old to experience.

I am sharing this with you to paint a picture for where we are headed in this book. Let me say that because of how I hated my life and my situation, I had thoughts of suicide. My first suicide attempt was in the 6th grade. No one knew about it. After coming from P.E., I was depressed about my life so I dropped to the floor directly on my head. I laid there with a concussion until I was brought to the office. When the EMT arrived, I felt like I was going to die. So I wanted to receive it, and go where the bright light church folks talked about was; but I never saw it. I literally checked out of life. I wanted to be dead and I wasn't responding to the EMT, so they rushed me to the hospital. They put an IV in me while I was in the ambulance. It was very cold that day. I remember this because they did not cover me up at all when they were carrying me. Why would I want to be dead? Was it because of my depressive state and thoughts about suicide that made me want to die? Turns out that a heat stroke caused all this to happen.

As I began to review life as an adult, many memories came to light. Sharing these things with you has not been easy, but I assure you that if you can survive the worst of life's tribulations, you will enjoy the fruit of life's triumphs. There was a time in class when I brought a scrapbook that had all of my dad's stuff in it. There were pictures from when he played in college and letters from pro scouts. I recall being proud to show this off, although, at the time, he was not around. One day, I put it in my cubby hole under my desk. Roaches came out of it and scared all the students around me. The girls ran and the guys squashed them. My nickname became "Roach." I guess what hurt me most wasn't the kids that laughed, but the teacher who laughed at me. I watched her laugh at me in disgust. She never tried to take over the situation and calm down the class. I felt like the laughter would never end. I was the tallest person in the class and I felt just as small as the roaches coming out of my book. As a young man, I was ashamed. I hated myself and I didn't have many friends. There were ones who pretended to be my friend when I had my drum out because I would let them play. I was what you would call a loner or an outcast. I always rolled solo in my own little world. Never felt accepted in any clique or group. Should I have been angry? Did I have a reason to be at this point?

Well, we had to move because we could not keep up with the bills. Our only hope was to go to a battered women's shelter. My mother had to say that she was in hiding from her boyfriend in order for them to help us. We stayed until the time had expired and then she decided to transfer to yet another shelter. We stayed there until that time ended, and then we were out on the street with nothing but the choice to go right or left with our trash bags full of stolen clothes. It seemed we had no hope left. Weren't there people out there who could help? Were we supposed to go to back to the mission? Shortly after all this was when my grandfather died. This struggle was an ongoing cycle that kept going and going like one big nightmare that I would one day wake up from. But being in it, the nightmare is thick. There are hardly any memories of me smiling as a child. I can barely remember joy. As the anger and hatred filled those moments, I could not fully enjoy happy events. I may never get those years back, but they have led me here: to speak about my experience. To understand my anger, how to use it, how it uses me, and how to respond appropriately.

ALL ABOUT YOU

If you have read the introduction of my book, you were able to spend a little time reading about my life. I wanted you to know that I am only human just like you. We all have a story with dreams and aspirations in life that we want to achieve. Don't worry we will get to the anger stuff but right now, I want you tell me about your dreams in life? What inspires you? Who inspires you? What are your goals?

Write down your dreams:

Did you once have any dreams? Thoughts of what you wanted to be? Maybe a doctor, professional athlete, music artist, photographer or have your own business? Did you ever want to achieve a higher level education, whether it was a GED, PhD or just do something great while here on earth? What do you really want? (Explain)

_____

_____

_____

_____

_____

_____

_____

_____

_____

_____

_____

_____

_____

_____

What/Who inspires you? (Explain)

_____
_____
_____
_____
_____
_____
_____
_____
_____
_____
_____
_____
_____
_____
_____
_____
_____
_____
_____

What are your goals in life? (If you don't know how to set goals yet, just explain the best you can)

_____
_____
_____
_____
_____
_____
_____
_____
_____
_____
_____

Is there anything "good" in your life at the moment or can you remember a time when you smiled with joy? (Explain)

_____
_____
_____
_____
_____
_____
_____
_____
_____
_____
_____
_____
_____
_____
_____
_____
_____
_____
_____
_____

What do you think about yourself today? (Be real and truthfully honest)

_____
_____
_____
_____
_____
_____
_____
_____

26

Creative Space

You are probably wondering why you are writing all this. Well, I wanted you to look deep inside yourself and see light somewhere in your life. I don't know where you are in your life right now but I need you to hope and dream again. This is a process, so be patient with yourself and take your time answering the questions.

CAUTION: The following chapter is a flashback in a moment in time when I released my anger to the universe. It may be a bit of a ruff ride.

THE LOVE OF ANGER

THOUGHTS OF AN ANGRY MAN:
FLASHBACK 2007

HEAR MY ROAR!

"See God I don't need your dang help or your words or wisdom and knowledge! Yeah, I'm pissed off!! Where in the world were you when I needed you!? Did you not get the prayer I sent!? I made sure to send it as a high priority!? Do you even exist!? Don't worry though, I've got anger. I'm in a rebound relationship with anger and I couldn't be happier. We go everywhere together. We're never apart. It's like we are one in the same. We speak the same language. Anger holds my hand when I'm threatened or in need. Anger builds me up with unbelievable power and support. This love has friends like my buddy Ego. Our friend Pride sometimes hangs out with us, too. When I'm down and out and feeling depressed or pain, anger's love is always there to comfort me. I understand that no one loves me the way anger does and anger doesn't care about whether I'm different. Anger doesn't bother about my race, religious beliefs, politics or social status. I have filled my heart up with this love of anger, and it's become my one true companion. I am born again, baptized in rejection, hatred and rage. I sent myself to die and be crucified. I have a new type of flesh called anger, for I will never be what I once was made. How about that? How do you like me now? Anger IS love, I AM anger and I AM god!

As I flashed back into time to describe my innermost thoughts, I bet you're probably wondering what in the world I'm talking about? I was in a lost dark place in my life and thought I was losing my absolute mind. I was confused on what the truth was.

I didn't know the creator of the universe and of all things I had no clue of who I was. I was tired and angry at the world.

Growing up I felt rejected and not loved by my parents, and the world. All I really wanted was to be happy and loved. Is that so hard to come by? Someone to love you, spends time with you, and show that you care? I hated who I was and failing to become the person I know I am inside. Suicide seemed like a clever option. It felt like an exit sign to all the pressures of life: no money, no job, no dreams, no hope, and no light to be found in sight. I was lost in this dark place and I needed to know I was valuable, loved and worthy of living. So, I said angrily to myself, "I need to love me. I'm the only one who cares anyway." It was fueled by this anger, this hatred of the world and God and everything. Anger was all I felt in my heart, and more than that, it gave me a sense of power. My relationship with anger was growing and developing daily; it was the only consistent force in my life, and for that, anger felt reliable. In my mind, I believed that anger and I were identical. I thought that I would simply not exist without it. In my rage and rejection, I birthed a new god in my mind, a god I could understand, a god who was there for me. Me! Isaac, the god of anger!

I want you to see my thoughts, my visions, my pain, and some moments in my life. This is raw and real life for some of us; we live and breathe this love called anger. We worship this strong emotion. Anger is a god in our lives.

So, now do you believe you can love anger? Is it possible to love the way you feel? Do you love being happy or filled with joy? Do you love having money in your pocket?? Do you love your music? Do you love the hottest sneakers out? Do you love your sports or maybe your video games? If other people "love" the way they feel, whether it's a happy emotion, or a good sensational feeling, why can't I love anger? Is anger not an emotion? Is it not a feeling? What is love really? Is love patient? Is love kind? Is it an action? Is love a choice?

If negative anger is used for selfish gain it will not yield fruit. It holds a false sense of reality and the appearance of truth. We allow this emotion to reign in our lives. Let me ask you, are you worth fighting for? Do you believe you are valuable? Yes! Let me say that you are. You are here with me reading this book looking for a way out. You are looking for answers. Most people just don't understand what's really going on inside you. Is this depression you are experiencing? It thrives in privacy. Consider this book as your accountability partner, if you cannot find someone to talk to. In your honesty, and your quest for change, there Is nothing to fear. As you may have heard, fear is better summed up as, "False Evidence Appearing to be Real." It only exists if you allow it.

You say "Ooh, I'm not scared, Isaac. I'm tough." What makes you so tough? The fear you instill in everyone else around you, because they don't know when you're going to explode next? Is it your size that makes you unafraid, or your "whatever" attitude? Am I making you angry right now? Good. It's time to take inventory of your life, and all the "false evidence" you've used to build illusions about your worth that are not real. No matter how many fights you have won, the "street cred" you have, video games youhave, music artist you mimic or celebrity you follow on IG—whatever makes you feel on top—aren't enough. We're about to take a good, hard, look at the Truth of you, and uncover the purpose anger has been playing in your life.

WHAT IS THIS?

If you have made it to this chapter, you must be one angry individual. Let's get real with life now and get to some tools that will help you. What is anger exactly? Anger is a natural human emotion that everyone has experienced at one point in their lives or another. Webster's defines it as a strong feeling of displeasure and antagonism, indignation or an automatic reaction to any real or imagined insult, frustration, or injustice, producing emotional agitation seeking expression. To sum it all up, anger is a strong emotion. Do you agree? I like how my mentor explained anger. He said, "It is Allowing Negativity to Generate Emotional Rage (A.N.G.E.R.)." The most common cases and worldly views say that anger is negative. This is true, but bear with me as I explain some things you may not have thought about. As I told you earlier, for me anger "WAS" love. It was so very strong that it seemed I worshiped anger as god. If you have not experienced any of the stories I shared, you are blessed because you are not as jacked up as I was. Since I have shared some of my scars, I would like to ask you, what is your story? If this is too much, maybe you should return this book or give it to someone who lives an angry lifestyle. You can get some ice cream, (my favorite is Mexican vanilla with hot fudge on top) and be on your merry way. As for the rest of you, start writing this down. Invest in a spiral notebook or something dedicated to your anger. Serious students of life are always learning, so they need to always be prepared to take notes. If not, you are wasting your time and mine.

This sleeping giant, ladies and gentlemen, wakes up when a threat occurs, and an internal fight or flight response is activated. Usually this is a warning sign that something is going on and is a hindrance to you. When you are displeased, threatened, or straight-up angry. You can measure your anger to determine if it is too intense for too long or becomes more frequent aggression. Look out for what I call the cousins of anger: fear, rejection, pride. Pride comes before a fall. Beware of your ego because it can take you to unbelievable heights and then drop you as fast as the law of gravity will allow. For me, I believe the power of anger can be activated by fear and pride. Pride motivates or provokes anger to a very dangerous level. Fear creates a sense of uncertainty and we are more prone to react versus act towards the situation. Look on the bright side, what you feared the most, you may now have the courage to stand up and face head on. Remember fear is only an illusion; therefore, it does not exist. It is challenging handling anger in love. It is equally difficult to manage anger without spreading it like wildfire.

I like that there are faces of anger: looking like you are constipated, that crazy lost stare, and that I hit my pinky toe on the edge of bed face. The muscles in your face form a certain arrangement to show these faces. I am pretty sure some of us have had all of these faces at one point or another. You may not know that you are making them, but they show and everyone can read your expressions. You may even think "I don't care. I'm not going to show emotion." In reality, you are showing emotion all the time, even when you are trying hard not to. It is natural for us to express ourselves. Some people know that I go into blank stares where it makes people uncomfortable. It's that "Rowe" look. They say that I look like I'm plotting to hurt someone. In truth, it is my "I'm processing" face; processing if I should respond—not react, but respond. And yet, my face still looks ominous to the people around me.

Hiding anger is the most dangerous, in my opinion. That is like an atomic bomb waiting to be initiated with the right trigger. It can destroy everything in a wide radius. So your parents and your friends are all in danger. This was most likely me. After I built a couple of little bombs, I released them on whoever was in my way. I have cursed my best friends, fighting over the littlest things with my "ride or die" brothers. Luckily, I am blessed to have real homeboys who are down with me through thick and thin. They know anger is a real struggle, a deep habit of being that takes time to examine, undo, and express healthfully.

You can probably relate to the blow-ups and outburst that I've experienced due to misplaced anger. There are three Greek words that describes anger. The first word Perogismos: repressed anger, or hidden anger. This type of anger is put into a box, comprised of many other angry thoughts sealed inside. This is what I call the hosting room of anger. It hosts anger, just waiting on the right moment to pull the trigger and release it into the atmosphere. It reminds me of when a person vomits and yesterday's old food comes to the surface. You say, "When did I eat corn, where did this come from?!" Yes, this can be shocking at the time because you may not know how to control such measures of anger. It's kind of like when someone is constipated. Maybe they ate too much, and it's been backed up a while, and when it finally comes out, it's not pretty at all.

This is what repressed anger is like. It's been backed up for a while. And it's definitely not pretty. So when you realize that you hide or repress anger, ask yourself, "Am I angrily constipated?" The second word is Orgay, the most natural and common anger. Being angry for normal everyday things is okay, but be careful not to let it continue into the next day if you can. Plus, it is not worth being angry all day, it takes too much of your time and energy. If you don't realize, time is a limited resource. You cannot replace another person and you cannot add more time to your life, or pause it, or even rewind it. It's always on play.

If you have a beef with your homeboy or sister girl, squash it. To be real with you, tomorrow isn't promised for any of us. I remember having bad dreams and nightmares about strange things like running and people shooting at me, wanting me to die.

Everything was destroyed around me, with no people in sight. I felt like I was by myself and no one was here for me. Why should I be here? Caution! That's a suicide knock!

The third word for anger is Thumos, which is my favorite. It is an explosive temper or outburst of rage. I exploded many times in my life. I allowed myself to feel rejected, unloved, depressed, jealous, angry, prideful, fearful, shameful and embarrassed about my life. Can you relate? Have you ever exploded on someone? If so, can you remember why you did? Anger can take over your life and consume every bit of you if you allow it and fail to stand firm. Yes I said it if you allow it to control you; it doesn't care about anything but itself. No more excuses now. Excuses are for people who support and perpetrate incompetence. Maybe you're a young man or young lady and you have had feelings and thoughts like you would never finish high school or college. "Your parents didn't make it, so what makes you so different? Everyone is smarter than you and besides you don't deserve friends. You don't fit in or belong." As I shared with you earlier, I didn't particularly like not being able to fit in, but I liked to think I wasn't born to fit in anyway. I was born to stand out. We all want to feel accepted and loved in some form or fashion. The reality is if people can't accept you for who you are, then you don't need to be hanging with them anyway. You have to be in maturity and say, "I'm responsible for my own actions. I have control over my thoughts, and if it is not the truth, I'll cast it out!" Meaning I'm not going to let this thought come in and interrupt my peace. It is our perception of a situation or an event that creates anger, which is the cognitive trigger. There is a natural sense that we all have that signals caution and judges whether an event is threatening or not. Your trigger thoughts can produce arousal, which activates your internal fight or flight response. I want you to understand from a different perspective of what anger has been and still is in my life. I don't want to bore you with all the physiological and psychological stuff, but I encourage researching it for yourself. There are a lot of self-help books and people with PhD's who are probably qualified on paper, but there is something that they are missing. They do not really understand serving a life sentence in anger prison. To experience anger in different aspects and depths cannot be explained in words only. It is a feeling, like love, that can only be known. In my opinion, anger is derived from the meaning and value you place on it that gives it life.

So I ask myself, what is this? What is this I am feeling that makes me want to knock people out? What makes me want to throw people out the window? Here is a story about a time when I was working at a shipping company while attending college. I worked about four years total and I did not leave on good terms. I became a rage-aholic in that place. I was learning who I was, what I was doing, and hating how life had dealt me this hand. [Let me pause for a second to let you know because I didn't face my challenges head on or didn't tell anyone about what's going on with me, I made more mistakes as I got older.] I hated myself and wanted to know why did I have to go through so much pain and heartache. I had to learned that the world can be a very cruel and evil place. They wrote me up plenty of times but it really didn't faze me. I had now reached a seniority spot where I was good in placement. I was one of the hardest workers. They didn't fire me even after I cursed out the bosses and got in their faces. I didn't do anything they said when I was angry. Yes, they were very afraid of that boy Rowe. Trust me; they knew I would catch them in the streets. The workers said that they didn't want to work with me because I was crazy. I thought yeah, well, I'm only a smidge, as I said with a smile. Although I was good at what work I did, they didn't want to fire me or to risk being hurt or punked out in front of the employees. It got to a point where they put me on last chance agreement where I had to go to a therapist for my anger. They said I was a hazard to the work environment. Employees complained that nobody wanted to work around me. Wow, are you serious? You messing with my money now, hold up! It was funny to me at first, because I didn't really realize I was that bad until the psych doctor said I was in great depression. That was causing my anger. They tried to get me on Prozac. Like for real, seriously? "I ain't taking that stuff! There's nothing wrong with me!" I was so in denial and blind to the truth that there was something going on. I just didn't want anyone to see it. Hey, does this sound familiar to you? I knew that I needed to one day understand about this strong emotion, my struggle and this condition I was in, but I was not really ready for the truth. To best honest, I was afraid of the truth, and what it had to say about me. Besides that, I was confused on what the truth really was. Did I listen to the truth? No, I did not. What I did know how to do was party, cover my issues with a mask and pretend to be someone I'm not. "I'm young! I got plenty of time and besides you only live once! YOLO, right?" Man, did those words hurt to say. What I said to myself is that I was not ready to be mature and accept responsibility at that time. Side bar: You young people think that the people around you don't know what they're talking about. But they care about you and are speaking the truth to you. Hear me; don't make the mistakes I did. That's why I am here having this conversation with you because, like those people, I care about you. Yes, you only live once, but don't make bad decisions based on limited information. This will lead you into a very dark place that you can't get yourself out of. Maybe you are out in the streets partying, being disrespectful, not doing homework or hanging out late with troublemaker friends like you lost your dang mind has consequences. You can't blame your lack of control on anything or anyone. FYI: that judge is not going to lock that "thing" or person who told you to do it. Guess who he/she will lock up instead? You! I must be real with you, I was no saint now. Yeah, I did that too. I'm am telling you from experience. This is not to scare you, but only to educate you about what is real out here in the world. Let's be smart about this, okay?

Anger is a strong emotional response and is usually activated when you feel rejected, fearful, have missed a specific goal or lost something you valued. Maybe you have an overly high expectation of something? We have been given this emotional response for righteous purposes. It is the fight within us. Some may call it righteous indignation. It is okay to be angry; it only depends in what context and how you act upon it. Yes, there are a lot of crazy information on the internet that say a lot about anger, but anger does have its place. Righteous anger can arise from a positive and correct perspective to handle situations. Even though anger is often dangerously harmful, anger can be good and used in a healthy way. Authors of "What's Good About Anger" Ted Griffin and Lynette Hoy writes, "Anger, though potentially harmful, can be transformed into a positive force accomplishing great good in our lives." Anger can produce much fruit. I founded an organization called "The Man In Me", out of my anger for the men and the fatherlessness in America. If you didn't know, anger is translated in other Greek meanings like passion or energy; others mean agitating or boiling. So I was angry about this when I saw so many men not taking their role as men and fathers. In my curiosity, I thought that there must be something behind this behavior. So, like Gandhi said, I wanted to be the change I wanted to see, also to help other men, fathers and their families. My anger for the cause drove me to a desire and passion to help serve others. There you go! Is that not healthy fruit? So that's why I can say from my own experience that not all anger is bad; there are some healthy uses for anger. Let's be real. Nine times out of ten, when a situation or event occurs, and anger is pulling from inside, it's a prideful a little "it's all about me and no one else." It's the "me" show, and how "I" feel, and how this is actually making "me" feel right now. If you take a good look around, people are resulting to violent behavior over the dumbest, idiotic excuses ever. Some of these parents are losing their dang minds, hurting their own children. People are fighting because someone accidentally stepped on their shoes or because of rumors. Come on now! Really!? Is this where we are as a people? We are hurting ourselves!

Anger has been around for a long time now but people are getting all brand new with it like it just arrived. I believe it's time to put a stop and say, "Enough already! I'm sick and tired of being this way. I have allowed anger to destroy my relationships with my friends, my parents, even my teachers." It's so exhausting being angry and holding all this weight that we were never meant to carry. So how do we let it go?

What is Anger?

It is a strong feeling or an intense emotional state of displeasure and antagonism, indignation or an automatic reaction to any real or imagined insult, frustration, or injustice, producing emotional agitation seeking expression. It is also described in Greek as passion, energy, boiling and wrath.

I want you to know this emotion is natural and apart of you like all the other emotions you feel on the day to day basis.

(Read *What is this?*)

After reading *What is this?*)in your own words, is anger positive or negative to you?

_____
_____
_____
_____
_____
_____
_____
_____
_____
_____
_____
_____

How have you used anger in a unhealthy way? (Ex. Verbal or Physical attacks, throw or break, or yell or scream)

_____
_____
_____
_____
_____

_____

_____

_____

_____

_____

_____

_____

_____

_____

_____

How have you used anger in a healthy way? (Ex. Defending your family, Used it as motivation to reach goals.)

_____

_____

_____

_____

_____

_____

_____

_____

_____

_____

_____

_____

What do you think makes you angry?

_____

_____

_____

_____

_____

How do you feel when you are experiencing this strong emotionof anger? (Describe)

_____

_____

_____

_____

What happens when you feel anger or angered at something/someone?

_____

_____

_____

_____

_____

_____

_____

_____

When angry, are you silent, do you fight back, or start screaming or cursing? (Describe)

_____

_____

_____

_____

_____

Do you _regret_ anything you did while you were angry?

_____

_____

_____

Do you ever feel guilty or bad about something you did or said while angry? (Describe)

_____

_____

_____

_____

_____

_____

_____

_____

Have you asked yourself, What is really going on in this situation?" If not, why?

_____

_____

_____

_____

_____

_____

What can or could you do to overcome this situation?

_____

_____

_____

_____

_____

_____

_____

_____

How do you manage your anger?

_____

_____

_____

_____

_____

Do you have any techniques to calm down?

_____

_____

_____

_____

_____

_____

_____

_____

_____

_____

_____

_____

_____

_____

_____

ANGRY ROOTS

AKA "HIDDEN THINGS"

What is it that made you angry? Was it someone or something? A series of circumstances? I can tell you one thing: you weren't born angry. I have come to realize that our thoughts and what we believe is what makes us angry. Dr. Matthew Mckay says "There is nothing automatic about getting angry. Pain does not make you angry. Thoughts make you angry; beliefs and assumptions make you angry." There is something that we are missing which we can't see on the surface. Is this derived from the past or is it a current situation? When did anger become an issue for you, as a child, as a teenager or young adult? If you really want to understand this emotion, begin to discover the root of the anger. I know you don't want to dig up any old stuff or think about those things you have masked over for years now, but it helped me. We can do anything we put our minds to do. Okay, Let's stop making excuses! All they do is support your false incompetency. I don't want to talk to people who throw hissy fits because your parents gave you less allowance this week, or upset your favorite shoes got dirty. Yes, that's true, natural anger. I don't doubt you aren't angry. The truth be told, it's much deeper than that and you know it. You probably don't have peace in your life, and you're addicted to drama. Maybe you think your life is peachy and perfect, but you're here with me. I was the same way too. I easily grew bored and wanted to spice things up a bit. Everyone has a story and it is hidden so deep in your mind that it's only felt, not identified. These are repressed thoughts and emotions that I call "Hidden Things." If there is an infection, we must show and identify where the pain or wound is, so that we can start the healing process. If not, then covering up and hiding the wound only creates an infection. Then the infection spreads throughout your life. Something so small as a cut can end up as a major infection.

There is a reason behind every behavior that someone displays. For example, recognizing what triggers your anger is like discovering the branches to a tree whose roots are hidden beneath the surface. If you ever noticed that an old tree has roots that are deep and spread underground. The older trees have such deep roots. It took years upon years to grow deeper and deeper into the ground. It's like those "hidden things" that you push down, out of sight and out of mind. You don't want to say anything because you really don't know how to deal with it to be honest, right? And what if you express it? Does it make you weak or will you have changed who you are because of it? I have gotten used to being in that state of mind; it gave me a false sense of identity and the appearance of truth, like we discussed earlier. During your travels in life from place to place, you have probably picked up some type of luggage in your journey. This may be some luggage that you packed up with roots embedded inside. This luggage or baggage you now carry gets expensive to travel with when you have a multitude of items such as fear, rejection, insecurity, self-esteem, pride, poverty, depression, suicide, and abuse inside. Everywhere you go it's a hindrance and is always difficult to move around. Yeah, trust me, it's a dysfunctional way to live but I chose to carry it because I didn't know how to get rid of it. I didn't understand why I carried it. I just knew that I would carry it until I figured it out. I learned to conform to it rather than be free of it. I adjusted it however I needed, to balance and walk with this limp of dysfunctional unhealthiness. Besides, I'm a grown man. I have got to keep it moving right? I'm supposed to be tough, a soldier; I ain't no punk! Everywhere I go, I have to check into the secret hotel. This is where I'm only accepted: me and my "luggage." It's usually sitting all alone by me unless I see others who carry the same baggage. Since we are here on the subject, let's reveal what was in the luggage shall we? Real talk. I was rejected by girls growing up because I thought I wasn't handsome enough or because I didn't have the money, certain status or didn't hang with the "cool" club to talk to them.

As I got older, I remember not being able to speak to ladies due to my own insecurities, and my fear of rejection. I hated being the "nice guy" so I created a beast. I put on a facade to hide the true me because it's easier to pretend to be someone else. Nobody really liked the old me anyway. I never had many friends. In my day, if you didn't smoke, have a luxury car, or have a lot of money, you couldn't get the females. I had to perfect my mouth piece and build this false self-esteem so that I could date any girl I wanted. My mindset was, "I don't want to be a loser anymore. I want to be somebody special that the people will like." I see this in the music industry and in professional careers; people forget who they are and become what society wants them to be. I will not go deep into this. It is not worth it, trust me. There are consequences for being irresponsible. It's sad, really I needed to find myself because every day I was losing my identity more and more, masking what was underneath: "angry roots." My cry for help was going unnoticed. It seemed nobody cared, so why should I? I didn't know how to deal with all the repressed and suppressed emotions. Sometimes we are considered weak if our emotions are expressed, when being vulnerable and having the ability to release all that strong emotion is exactly what we need. I screamed, yelled and cursed at the sky. That was probably not the best thing to do, but that's exactly where I was at. This reason behind my behavior came to light. I could not allow myself to be in total darkness anymore. This anger prison almost got the best of me.

In my middle school days, during the time of gangs. Back then, my family and I lived from place to place: the mission, the battered women's shelter, the Salvation Army, and on the streets. Just to let you know, this was not hood stuff or street life, this was poverty. My mother was a drug addict and struggled with her stronghold. Some guys came into the neighborhood to help and inspire the underprivileged kids and to teach the game of football. You know I had a little bit of an arm, so I figured I'd try out for the team. The coaches didn't put me in as quarterback but I was on the offensive line. To make a long story short, we took physicals, practiced and prepared for everything. When the first game came up, the coaches lined everyone up and called out where we going to be..."You, you, ah...you, but not you (pointing at me)!" I'm like "What? Not me!? They said, "Yeah, you're too big." My 12-year-old mind didn't understand how "big" became a bad thing for football. I remembered feeling so crushed, isolated and unwanted by that. My thought was, "I thought you were here to help us? This is my only hope to escape my life at home." It was going to be an escape from the drug dealers coming in and out of my home. One time, they came in my house and tried to kill everyone in my family. Yeah, this is real life in the streets. My two brothers were ten and two at the time. My thoughts were, "I'm the man of the house; I'm the big brother; I'm responsible and I cannot protect them." I'm not telling you this so you will give me pity party or feel sorry about why Isaac had to go through that. I'm sharing my life with you and this is real for me. Just be grateful it wasn't worse or it wasn't you! Remember we are discovering the hidden things, the angry roots of what is causing the life of anger. So as I continued to open my luxury signature series hidden things luggage set, I dug deeper. Could my grandfather passing away be a root? He was my rock, everything to me, my papal. This is the man who believed in me when I didn't believe in myself. He taught me how to play baseball when I was the worst on the team. He molded me into one of the best players. I told you earlier that he was involved in a car accident and died on the way to the hospital. I am reminded every day by those electronic signs off the Texas highways of the accidental automobile death toll. I was angry because my grandfather was gone and I did not know what to do. I felt abandoned. The love I had known to be real was no longer. Yeah, it still hurts today. We sometimes get so angry when we want things to go our way. We want to have control over situations. We have no control over death. It is a part of life.

The first time I attempted suicide was in the 6th grade; I was at a crossroads. CDC (Centers for disease control and prevention) show that for youth between the ages of 10 and 24, suicide is the third leading cause of death. It results in approximately 4,600 lives lost each year. As the teen suicide rate is rising, today society can relate why they feel the way they do. As you know, I had a mother with an addiction and she had an abusive boyfriend. At that time, I felt that there was no hope. I had been laughed at and bullied at school, not only by the students, but even by a teacher. Oh how embarrassed and ashamed I was to be alive! Sticks and stones may break your bones but words will never hurt you is far from the truth. Sticks and stones can hurt me but the power of negative words can kill me If I believed it to be true. In my adolescent mind, I thought there was no light, no options to choose from, only pain and depression for me. I thought the only way to stop this pain from hurting was to take my own life. After all, I was worthless and nobody cared or loved me. Why not? The only peace for me was the walk from home to school and from school to home. This was a very long walk with my sticks in one hand and my snare drum in the other. What was the point of life? Why did this to happen to me? Sidebar: If you are a teenager or adult that's dealing with these feelings, first know that you are valuable! I'm still here and we will get through this together, just hold on! Suicide is not worth it.

As I kept digging deeper to the roots of anger, I realized that abuse was very foundational of my life… Could it be that the angry root and prison was built from the mental and verbal abuse that my mother put my brothers and me through? Perhaps when I was at the tender age of six years old, I had already been touched inappropriately by an adult female and male? When my parents chose to go out and party, they hired "babysitters" that they barely knew to watch us. As tears run down my face, I express to you this was very uncomfortable to speak about. I woke up early one day to play with leftover firecrackers after being "touched". I set a small mattress on fire that was beside a trash can. That led to setting a bunch of trees on fire. The fireman came to put the blaze out. If I had not been through enough already, my mother came and beat me with a broomstick for playing with fire. Can you tell me why would another grown man (male babysitter) would touch a boy and do things to him that would take his innocence and confuse him? I can remember the smell of cheap soap as he did things to my 6-year-old boy body. The horror seemed like it would never end. This happened multiple times and it hurts too much to count. It was like time and space froze and I was being punished for something I had no understanding about. Am I not a boy!? Is this right? Growing up, I started asking myself questions about my masculinity, my sexuality and what was wrong with me. Why did I feel so guilty and ashamed? I asked myself, "Am I gay now, and do I have disease like they talk about on the news?" Why would someone manipulate a child like this? He threatened to do this to my younger brother as well, if I chose not to do what he said. I tried to fight for myself, but he said he would tell my parents what I did. He played upon my shame and my guilt, telling me that I am wrong for what I did. Because I knew this was so wrong, and I felt deep inside it wasn't right. I was afraid to mention it. I just didn't want my parents or anyone to know about this. Something is wrong, somebody anybody help me!! Every time I said no, as tears run down my face, I could not stand to watch as he grabbed my brother to take him into the bathroom to do it to him too if I didn't. So I gave in. I'm his big brother and it's my job to protect him. My brother was only three years old!

It's crazy how a traumatizing moment can affect your life and the lives of others. As I got older. I hated my parents. I hated my family. I hated myself. My question I would ask, as I looked up in the sky, why did this happen to me? Why me?" It took years upon years to search deep down into the depths of my repressed emotions to dig up the roots and that old luggage I had been carrying around. This weight I was never meant to carry around affected many aspects of my life because I didn't know how to deal with it. Sometimes it is very difficult to express emotions and feelings. Some things we would rather take to our grave than be healed, or let anyone know about the hidden things. For a long time, I lived as a victim, but now, after taking my power back, I am a victor. To tell you my hidden things, it took everything. I mean it took everything in me to tell this untold story. I'm still alive; I'm still here; I'm still standing strong! It's all on you now! What's your story? What's your hidden things? What are your "angry roots"? Let's open that luggage you have been carrying around that you don't know what to do with.

You want to know whom you truly and fully are inside, right? You have been holding in all types of offenses, anger, pride, rejection, resentment, fear and hatred. These feelings are keeping you from truly experiencing who you are. Let's take responsibility of our lives today! You have the power to change and to create whatever you want. I know you want to live what's inside you. It is possible, you know? You have to believe that it is. You may not feel like it will ever get better. You just can't help the way you feel, but I need you to believe again. I need you to have faith if you want to be free of everything that's holding you back from being healed of offences in life. They say insanity is doing something over and over again and expecting the different results. Let's change the way we think about the past and current situations. It's our perception that's jacking us up. We are such emotional creatures and it's natural to feel this way. This is what makes us human. The first thing I did was accept what happened to me. I stopped denying and fighting what really happened that was stirring up my anger. I had to really be honest with myself. I took off all my facades and roles I played.

I revealed my scars and wounds that never were fully healed. I got naked with the truth and I embraced it. I received that this really did happen. I cried and cried, because it was kind of anger that hurts. I hurt because I felt this pain but I was angry that I didn't know what to do with it. You don't have to do anything. Just sit there and get it all out. Release everything that is inside you! Release it! Say what you need to say, and how you really want to say it! I said it when I was alone, but you can definitely have someone with you during this time. I released my anger and the people who pissed me off, offended me, violated me or abused me in any kind of way! Maybe you are like me and it's your mother and father that caused your anger. You wished you had the two of them together like a real family. Maybe you wished things were different growing up. You would have loved to grow up in a nice neighborhood and not a poor one. Maybe you wished you actually had a childhood. You wished that you could have been what you were supposed to be at your age. Maybe you lost someone you loved dearly, who didn't deserve to die. You thought they would live forever. Only you know what your hidden things are. Now, did I do this all in one day? No, I didn't. It took several years of releasing and accepting the hand I was dealt in life. Repetition brings reinforcement, so I thought differently daily, released my anger daily. As I began to speak life over and over again, in time, the anger became less and less intense.

What are the "hidden things" that makes you angry?

_____

_____

_____

_____

_____

_____

_____

_____

_____

_____

_____

_____

_____

_____

_____

_____

_____

_____

_____

_____

_____

In the book I say that there are controlled and uncontrollable circumstances that make you angry but it's your thoughts. How you think or have a view or opinion about it. How you value or dislike something strikes a chord in your mind and your perception of the situation creates this strong emotion.

What really hurt you the most about these hidden things (dig deep)?
Someone or something? Explain..

_____

_____

_____

_____

_____

_____

_____

_____

_____

_____

_____

_____

_____

_____

_____

_____

_____

_____

_____

_____

_____

_____

_____

_____

_____

_____

_____

_____

_____

How long have you been dealing with this?

(Days, weeks, months, years?)

_____
_____
_____
_____
_____
_____
_____
_____
_____
_____

When did anger become an issue for you? (as a child or teenager or young adult?)
Was it from your past or current situation?

_____
_____
_____
_____
_____
_____
_____
_____
_____
_____
_____
_____
_____
_____
_____
_____
_____

EXPRESSIONS OF ANGER

I know you don't want to dig up any old stuff or think about those things you have masked over for years now, but it helped me. Everyone has a story and it is hidden so deep in your mind that it's only felt, not identified. These are repressed thoughts and emotions that I call "Hidden Things."

What FEELINGS do you experience?

For Example: irritated, fear, confused...

Angry Roots AKA "Hidden Things"- What's inside your luggage?

This luggage or baggage you now carry gets expensive to travel with when you have a multitude of items such as fear, rejection, insecurity, self-esteem, pride, poverty, depression, suicide, and abuse inside

The first thing I did was accept what happened to me. I stopped denying and fighting what really happened which was stirring up my anger. I had to really be honest with myself. I took off all my facades and roles I played. I revealed my scars and wounds that never were fully healed. I got naked with the truth and I embraced it. I received that this really did happen. I cried and cried, because it was kind of anger that hurts. I hurt because I felt this pain but I was angry that I didn't know what to do with it. You don't have to do anything. Just sit there and get it all out. Release everything that is inside you! Release it! Say what you need to say, and how you really want to say it!

Now Write!

_____

_____

_____

_____

_____

_____

_____

_____

_____

_____

_____

_____

_____

_____

_____

_____

_____

_____

_____

_____

_____

_____

After writing down everything, you may or may not feel better and it may not change your situation but this is a part of the training. Again, be patient with yourself and know that I am proud of you for taking the step to put in the work and invest in your well-being. Continue to write more or use the creative space to draw pictures to express your anger.

Creative Space

THE SYSTEM

I gave you my angry roots in my life that have been a stronghold and have kept me prisoner for many years. I hope you just discovered some of the roots in your life as well. This is a process in life where you must be patient and practice managing anger in your daily walk. This is not one of those overnight "look at me... all better" type of ordeals. Anything that is slow cooked, especially a nice, Texas style brisket, always turns out better and more satisfying. Before I get to the second point after releasing the truth, there is a system I put in place that helps control my anger when it arises. Wait, wait, hold up. You are probably wondering, "Why did he go straight into this after that last chapter? Does it hurt to think about?" Yes! But I have to move forward and forgive those lives I attempted to destroy. Guess what? I'm alive to tell the tale. We will get into all of that later. We know that we are angry people. Once we are able to recognize anger when it approaches, and identify what the emotion really is, we can better manage it. Once we have some management tools, we can then have some options to choose from. First, is to become aware of yourself. It is very important when dealing with the strong emotion of anger, that you must have awareness. You must watch yourself, observe yourself, and study yourself. What happens when anger, your feelings, your emotions are breached? I found out what works for me. I put up a system in my mind that is kind of like firewall to keep any viruses from entering in.

This system consist of a family of filters that are put in place to help block out any impurities and test whether or not this is good or bad, positive or negative. To setup your custom protection system, you must have the foundational setup.

The eye and ear gate filter, the trigger phase, the master control, and switching station. Next, is the emotional intelligence processing center, the distortion phase, and the outage called the blackout.

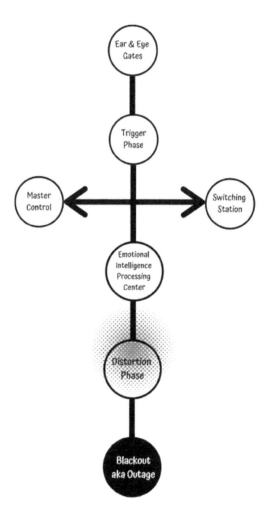

The external senses that are vital to be on watch are your ear and eye gates. Whatever you hear can affect how you think and perceive things. For example, certain types of music, especially in this day and age, are toxic to your mind. The music tricks you into believing things that are false. Some pretend and imitate to be like the musical artist when they themselves are not authentic, just pretenders. What you hear can alter the system on what you believe and you may not realize it at all. Be sure to guard your heart. There are people that are intentionally out to hurt you, because they are hurt, so you must be aware and stand guard over what enters inside. What you open your eyes to see and expose yourself to, generally becomes your reality.

Don't forget to be cautious of negative, toxic people and things on television that do not move you in a positive direction. Today, we have a lot of negative things in our society. The news is so depressing. It's always who died, what the celebrities are doing and politics. I just don't need this in my life especially after a hard day's work or school. Commercialized negative music on the radio. For a change, could I hear a song that's actually uplifting and inspiring? There's also a lot on social media and television which is believe to be inappropriate for the youth to see. So I try to be careful of what I watch and not surround myself around negative toxic people. These negative people always have something to about your creative idea or something you want to do for you. Negative people say things like, "you don't have any money to do that? You can't do that? Or why would you do that?" When I was around people who were negative and always had something to say about me, I got really angry. I got mad because, in all honesty, I really didn't know who I was and didn't know the truth about me. If you're not grounded and you don't know who you are, people can provoke you to move based on your emotions. You become emotional every time something happens and now you are considered sensitive. Negative, do-nothing people are not the people to surround yourself with. When you are around them, you now take on certain traits and some of their habits unknowingly. You may think you can block out their behavior and not be susceptible to their influence, but it's impossible: humans are the greatest imitators. It's subconscious. It's how we show we are relating to one another. This negativity can spread and cause arousal or some other type of trigger. It may give you something false or bring up memories of those old scars from the past that you didnot let go of. In this stage, you should start to be aware of yourself, of what is happening to you mentally, spiritually and physically. Are you sweating? Are your fists starting to clench? Is your heart rate increasing? In this stage, it's possible to cast out all the negativity and anger triggers, if you focus your mind outside of the trigger. When my triggers are ignited, I tell myself "Hey, let it go. I'm done! I have too much life to live and I don't have energy and time to be angry." We want to prevent this flow of anger from continuing to the trigger phase.

Ralph Waldo Emerson said that "For every minute you remain angry, you give up sixty seconds of peace of mind."

That leads me to my next stage in this system: the trigger phase. There are bodily and cognitive triggers. The bodily triggers are some like your diet, like sugars, are reportedly are not good. Are you getting proper nutrition, exercise, and sleep? Or are you always tired, sluggish, and unmotivated? Being tired like this leads to irritation. For example if you are tired and haven't had sleep, you might be irritable. You may not have as much tolerance as another day. If you are feeling ill or have some pain, you may be in a pre-angered state already. It's best to be active and eat healthier foods. Eating live foods, like vegetables and fresh meats, give you more sustainable energy than processed food, which has little to no nutrients. It is the "deadweight" of your diet, because it is basically a "dead" food. When you nourish your body, mind, and spirit, you can function every day and decrease the stress level, as well as the frequency of anger triggers. Personally, I go to the gym, hit the weights, or watch a good movie at the theatre. The cognitive triggers are the thoughts you think and perceive. This is your mental state of mind whether it is true or false. Your perception of an event or situation creates anger. This can also be unresolved family or personal issues. Triggers can even include those angry roots and hidden things that sometimes creep up when reminded of something familiar to your senses. The trigger phase detects that there is something related to the five senses, but doesn't know what exactly it is or whether it is positive or negative. There's a quote by Confucius that "He who says he can and he who says he can't are both usually right." If we are able to change the way we think about things, we can change our behaviors, our reactions, our relationships. Deepak Chopra states that, "Our minds influence the key activity of the brain, which then influences everything; perception, cognition, thoughts and feelings, personal relationships; they're all a projection of you." Our perception is now viewed differently in such a way that it ultimately changes our life and how we shape life. These triggers detect the positive as well. You may have righteous anger to have peace and justice in a situation. That's what I call that good fight anger. Anger is good when it is used to fight for what is right and to protect yourself. This is the lion in you that stands up to those offenses. This is a gift, but society can see it as a bad thing, since it is "ANGER." This is a part of your nature to be this way. It is all about how you operate in it.

The master control center and switching station consists of emotional, cognitive, physiological, behavioral and situational controls. As your anger rises, it receives a signal sent from the trigger phase saying "error;" it could not cast it out. Your brain control center detects how angry or pissed off am I? Whether this feeling is positive or negative? It measures how angry should I be at this point or how much value I placed on this emotion. Which then leads to the Switching Station that detects senses of anger it is. Is this feeling, a sense of justice and order, revenge or pride? How does this make me feel? What level of anger am I experiencing? Is it the mental state of mind that includes life and my cultural beliefs? Your thought life usually connects with biased information and your perceptions. Your thoughts make you become angry, whether or not you believe or assume things. This could be true or false, but it's your perception. Let me tell you, perception is one hell of a drug. I said earlier that it is the meaning and value that gives it life.

As we then enter in the Emotional intelligence filter, you are able to recognize your own feelings and manage your emotions. You should be able to understand your feelings and be able to make life decisions. You want to manage your life on a day to day basis knowing you have some tools in your belt. You don't have to keep everything inside causing you to implode or explode. I shared with you earlier that my angry roots began when I didn't find the hidden things that caused me to build up inside. It was too much to bear and had to be released, causing a flood of anger. You want to pay attention to people and have a little bit of empathy for them. I like how Daniel Goleman said, "A prerequisite to empathy is simply paying attention to the person in pain." They may not know what they are doing so sometimes you must be patient being sensitive to someone else's feelings and perspective. You want to take yourself out the situation to look at things from different outlook or perspective. So maybe if I had known this back then when I was tripping' on the job, I wouldn't have acted that way towards my co-workers and bosses. I didn't control myself nor did I care. I operated on how I felt every day. I loved the power it gave me, but in the same sense, I had no power at all. In this phase of your personal system, you must learn to be assertive. What does that mean? Well I'm glad you asked! It is standing up for your rights without being disrespectful. Confronting the issue at hand, not being afraid but being confident in the process. Yes, you are being bullied, your parents aren't getting along or maybe someone didn't pay you back like they said they would, but you don't have to curse them out and make ascene about it.

So, now it's time to take action and use "I" statements like, "I felt confused because you pushed me into my locker in between class. If you thought I was spreading rumors about, next time just come ask me directly ." Tell them what you don't like or what you would like to have happen in the matter. There's nothing wrong with expressing your feelings in a firm tone, stating the truth at hand. I must warn you about the cousin of anger called pride. It's very subtle and easy to slip in a self-righteous attitude. "How dare you do this to me! Do you know who I am?" All this is pride leading up to anger. Being puffed up and getting your chest all swollen up is now a pre-angered state. The more you think about it the more prideful you get and it goes right into anger. Then other hidden things come into play that have absolutely nothing to do with anything. The enemy loves this part.

It leads me to my next phase in the system which is the distortion phase. This is when you cannot fight in the emotional intelligence filter. Now your thoughts become clouded and distorted. You don't think clearly and as the fight or flight response is activated you get more aroused. You begin to see things in black and white and over exaggerate the negative events at hand. I usually jump to conclusions and assume everything possible but nothing positive. I am quick to cut people if they aren't with the program. Yes, I have tried to reason with positive thoughts but sometimes I loved being angry. My self-talk that is supposed to help me in this is broken because of the negative talk. So I feel like it's a good day to be angry. Why not? Let's do it! Besides, at the time, I had not dealt with anything in my past and I carried my heavy luggage around with me. So, I thought, let's unpack and stay awhile. I justified and validated my actions, felt sorry for myself, and wanted revenge. Those "why me" questions start to surface and pain is released to get the results I want. My pride got the best of me. First pride, then the crash; the bigger the ego, the harder the fall. Man did I fall! Pride will take you on a rollercoaster ride that goes up and drops off with no more tracks left. Gravity takes control. I fell hard into the last stage called the outage. Ever notice that in a storm that the lights may go out? Well, that's called an outage and there is no electricity. I want you to imagine that the light that was there went out and now I was in total darkness. This is the blackout. The blackout is when the Hulk comes out. This is the top level of rage. I am now a bomb ready go off with a blast radius of 50 feet. I have turned my anger into a weapon. Let me tell you, this is an out of body experience. I shared with you earlier that when I was married, I lost myself completely with all the drama, lies and adultery on both sides. The more I tried to get a grip on it by using anger to solve my problems, the more I lost control. It was like my spirit detached itself and my flesh took over my rage-filled actions. I'm inside realizing that this is not me at all; I'm asking myself, what's happening? I had to fight to calm down. As I was riding the rage wave, I began to breathe and began to self-talk, but at this point, it's too late. You want to start positive self-talk in the beginning, but be careful; the battle may be too thick to handle.

It took about an hour to calm down, come back into my body, and realize that what I just did was real. See, when a blackout or outage happens, all these things we discussed from the gates, to the triggers, to the distortion phase, to the blackout takes place your heart rate increases rapidly. You began to breathe harder and harder. Adrenaline is pumping into your body as it tells your brain to activate fight or flight response! As you get angrier, Thumos (the outburst) is in effect fully and oxygen leaves the brain only to narrow the scope down on the offense. You have no oxygen to think clearly and that's why it's distorted. It's cloudy and no anger management can be exercised. This is a system failure but don't beat yourself up about it. Learn from the system failures. Learn to fix the problem before it gets to that point.

I learned habitual anger over a long period of time. My view and outlook on life was cloudy or distorted. The only way to transform your mind is to replace negative thoughts with positive and set your mind to a new default. Remember, we have conditioned ourselves to be angry. People can change; you can change and I can change. Have I arrived at the place where I don't get angry? Absolutely not! I still get angry sometimes, but I work at it daily to manage my anger. It's not easy, and I rarely go into a rage or "Hulk" moment because I quickly calm myself down and manage it and express it healthfully, non destructive manner. Today you would never know how angry I was because of how well I'm able to manage it. I chose not to go through it or over it. I grew through the pain, the opposition, the guilt, the fear, the rejection, the pride and the resentment. After you understand the good and bad parts about anger, you will discover more of you and see what's inside you. I am still learning how to solve conflict in life and show empathy to others. I gave you my personal system and how I operate. Note this may not work for you but this is something that worked for me. Hopefully, you can take my life experiences and create your own system that works for you.

Once we have a few management tools there are more options to choose from! First, you have to become aware of yourself. It is very important when dealing with the strong emotion of anger, that you have awareness. You must monitor yourself, observe yourself and study yourself. What happens when anger, your feelings and emotions are breached? I found out what works for me and I put my own personal system place. It's kind of like a firewall in my mind that keeps any viruses from entering in. This system consists of a family of filters that are put in place to help block out any impurities and it will test whether or not the breach is positive or negative. To setup your custom protection system, you must have the foundational setup. The **eye** *and* **ear gate filter,** *the* **trigger phase,** *the* **master control,** *and* **switching station.** Next, is the **emotional intelligence processing center,** the **distortion phase,** and **the outage called the blackout.**

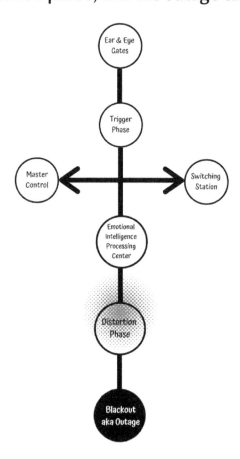

These filters should be in place so that strong emotions can be screened.

Eye Gates: **What do you expose your eyes to? What are you watching?**

_____

_____

_____

_____

_____

_____

Do you see anything different about yourself due to things you have allowed into your eye gates (why or why not)?

_____

_____

_____

_____

_____

_____

Is it positive of negative?

_____

_____

_____

Ear Gates: **What do you listen to and who do you listen to?**

_____

_____

_____

How does what you hear make you feel?

_____

_____

_____

Is it positive or negative?

_____

_____

_____

At this point in your workbook you should be more aware of yourself, and what is happening to you mentally, spiritually and physically. Are you sweating? Are your fists starting to clench? Is your heart rate increasing?

The next stage in this system: **The Trigger phase**. There are **Bodily** and **Cognitive Triggers.**

Bodily Triggers:

The bodily triggers such as your die, or sugars reportedly are not good. Are you getting proper nutrition, exercise, and sleep? Or are you always tired, sluggish, and unmotivated? Being tired like this leads to irritation. For example if you are tired and haven't had sleep, you might be irritable. You may not have as much tolerance for another day. If you are feeling ill or have some pain, you may be in a pre-angered state already. It's best to be active and eat healthier foods. Eating live foods, like vegetables and fresh meats, give you more sustainable energy than processed food, which has little to no nutrients. It is the "deadweight" of your diet, because it is basically a "dead" food. When you nourish your body, mind, and spirit, you can function every day and decrease the stress level, as well as the frequency of anger triggers.

What is your diet? (Describe)

_____

_____

_____

Are you getting proper nutrition, exercise, and sleep (If so how, if not why not?)

_____

_____

_____

Are you always (or often) tired, sluggish, and unmotivated (How does that feel, what do you think about it)?

_____

_____

_____

Do you feel healthy? What is "healthy" to you?

_____

_____

_____

The cognitive triggers are the thoughts you think and perceive. This is your mental state of mind whether it is true or false. Your perception of an event or situation creates anger. Triggers can even include those angry roots and hidden things that sometimes creep up when reminded of something familiar to your senses. The trigger phase detects that there is something related to the five senses, but doesn't know what exactly it is or whether it is positive or negative.

What are your thoughts day to day?

_____

_____

_____

_____

_____

What do you think about that which creates anger or boiling inside you?

_____

_____

_____

_____

_____

_____

Are you looking at the situation from all angles (what angles are you looking from?)

_____

_____

_____

_____

_____

_____

Could it be any of the issues mentioned above (if so which ones, if not why not?)

_____

_____

_____

Why do you care? What is it to you?

_____

_____

_____

_____

_____

Our perception is viewed differently sometimes in such a way that it ultimately changes our life and how we shape life. How is your perception (what is your perception?)

_____

_____

_____

_____

_____

_____

_____

_____

_____

_____

Can you cast out the thoughts? Can you get a different perspective? If so, how? What is the process?

_____

_____

_____

_____

_____

_____

_____

_____

As you are aroused in anger you now enter in the Master Control Center and Switching Station.

The master control center and switching station consists of emotional, cognitive, physiological, behavioral and situational controls. As your anger rises, it receives a signal sent from the trigger phase saying "error;" it could not cast it out. Your brain control center detects how angry or pissed off you are. Whether this feeling is positive or negative It measures how angry you should be at this point or how much value you place on this emotion.

How angry are you? (Explain)

_____
_____
_____
_____
_____
_____
_____
_____
_____

Is it positive or negative (why)?

_____
_____
_____
_____
_____

Depending on what you care about and the meaning/value you place on the emotions you are experiencing. You should be able to measure the priority of the feeling.

The Switching Station: … It detects the type of emotion coming in. **Is this feeling, a sense of justice and order, revenge or pride? Describe and explain.**

_____
_____
_____
_____
_____
_____
_____
_____
_____
_____
_____
_____

How does this make you feel?

_____
_____
_____
_____
_____
_____
_____
_____

Do your thoughts include your life and cultural beliefs (explain)?

_____

_____

_____

_____

_____

_____

_____

Your thought patterns usually connect with biased information and your perception. Your thoughts make you angry, whether or not you believe it or assume it. This could be true or false

Emotional Intelligence Filter: *At this phase you are able to recognize your own feelings and manage your emotions. You should be able to understand your feelings and be able to make life decisions. You want to manage your life on a day to day basis knowing you have some tools in your tool belt.*

In this phase of your personal system, you must learn to be assertive. What does that mean? Well I'm glad you asked! It is standing up for your rights without being disrespectful. Confronting the issue at hand, not being afraid but being confident in the process.

Define Aggressive:

_____
_____
_____

Define Passive:

_____
_____
_____

Define Assertive:

_____
_____
_____
_____
_____

In your own words what does assertive mean to you?

_____

_____

_____

_____

What is an example of a real life situation how you can be assertive and what would you do differently now than before?

_____

_____

_____

_____

_____

_____

_____

So, now it's time to take action and use "I" statements like, "I felt like you shouldn't have done that to me." Tell me what you don't like or what you would like to have happen in the matter. There's nothing wrong with expressing your feelings in a firm tone, stating the truth at hand.

*It leads me to my next phase in the system which is the **distortion phase**. This is when you cannot fight in the emotional intelligence filter. Now your thoughts have become clouded and distorted. You don't think clearly and as the fight or flight response is activated, you're more aroused. You begin to see things in black and white and over exaggerate the negative event at hand.*

Note: Remember to take deep breaths, continue self-talk and if you can take a walk to clear your head. Contact your accountability partner or close friend. I need you to see in the cloudiness and observe what is going on with you.

Are you confused in your thoughts at this point of anger?

_____

_____

_____

_____

_____

_____

Is there too much going on around you?

_____

_____

_____

_____

_____

Is there too much going on around you?

_____

_____

_____

_____

_____

Creative Space

Do you think you jumped to conclusions (how?)

_____

_____

_____

_____

What is the real truth?

_____

_____

_____

_____

_____

_____

Is what you are feeling worth it? Is it worth your life?

_____

_____

_____

_____

_____

_____

Let me answer that for you just in case, NO! It is not worth it!

*Ever notice that in a storm that the lights may go out? Well, that's called an outage and there is no electricity. I want you to imagine that the light that was there went out and now I was in total darkness. This is the **blackout.** The blackout is when the Hulk comes out. This is the top level of rage.*

See, when a blackout or outage happens, all these things we discussed from the gates, to the triggers, to the distortion phase, to the blackout takes place your heart rate increases rapidly. You began to breathe harder and harder. Adrenaline is pumping into your body as it tells your brain to activate fight or flight response! As you get angrier, Thumos is in effect fully and oxygen leaves the brain only to narrow the scope down on the offense. You have no oxygen to think clearly and that's why it's distorted. It's cloudy and no anger management can be exercised. This is a system failure but don't beat yourself up about it. Learn from the system failures. Learn to fix the problem before it gets to that point.

ALMOST THERE

How do you feel so far? I hope I didn't run you off with all the craziness, but this is raw and real life. Do you see yourself through my life and see some areas where you can identify where the strong emotions are coming from? We discussed many aspects of anger and dug deep to pull everything out onto the table. I am still here like I said I would be. I'm not going anywhere! Like I told you earlier, we are in this together. Ugly pasts, and all. As you know by now, my past ain't even close to pretty. But, it's part of my path; if we can start looking at the past as journey to freedom and understanding, there is hope for big change. Do you believe it's possible to break free from the prison you've built around yourself? When I released the truth into the atmosphere, that was the first step of m becoming free. The cell walls of my angry prison began to fall. There was nothing holding me back, but I had been there so long, I didn't want to leave. It was comfortable. Know that there's much more that takes place to be at a place of peace.

Don't worry we are getting to a close soon. The second aspect that I want you to know in this process of anger is the curse word forgiveness. Oh yes, forgiveness. But what is forgiveness, really? Is it even possible, and if so, who deserves it? YOU deserve it. First and foremost. By forgiving someone, you are setting YOURSELF free; therefore, forgiveness is a gift you give to yourself first, before extending it to anyone else. Forgiveness is possible and necessary for setting your anger free.

Let's dig into the details: Forgiveness is letting go of all the pain, heartache, people, situations, anger, bitterness, fear, shame, guilt, jealousy, pride, resentment and hatred that's in your heart. If you are like me, I was stuck in the past and didn't even know it. It took me 25 years of being angry and making many mistakes in life to realize what was going on with me. For some, the lesson is not so long; for others, it's longer. Things happened and I made bad choices that I take full responsibility for. I chose to act a fool and respond in such a crazy manner. There is no justification in this. You really want to know what I need you to find? Find a way to forgive the person who offended you. That person is living rent free in your head right now, because you are holding onto the rage they inspired. By "rent free," I am not saying that it is your job to go out and "make them pay." Basically, I am saying, you are paying, and paying hard, for allowing them to occupy your thoughts and emotions in such a destructive way. It causes YOUR blood pressure to rise. It causes YOUR muscles to tense. Meanwhile, the person who causes you so much fury is basically sipping on a fruit smoothie with an umbrella inside, smiling, having a good time. Who's being punished now? You are. And if you think your anger is a token, badge, or chip on your shoulder to allow you be ugly and bitter to people, I got news for you. You won't keep any type of relationship for long: love, family, friend, work, or even ones with your kids as you get older.

So do you feel justified now? That's your excuse for being ugly and bitter to people? We must not allow un-forgiveness to rule and govern our life. I understand the pain you feel. I understand you want other people to "pay" for your rage, and feel what you're feeling. You want revenge. You want "justice." But these desires are only further isolating; they cause more pain—to you, and the people you take your anger out on. You know this; you've seen how holding onto anger backfires in your face, how there is no selectivity in what it destroys; like a wildfire, it takes out everything. Because I've been in your shoes, I can say this confidently: more than revenge and justice, you want peace. True peace, and not the temporary satisfaction that comes with revenge tactics, only happens one way: through forgiveness. Can we agree today that forgiveness is something for you to at least attempt? Is your pride worth the price of freedom? The decision is yours to make. What is the worst that could happen? You become "soft" or "weak?" No. You become stronger than your rage. I studied forgiveness and I realized that I can't ask someone to forgive me when I can't forgive anyone else. So I had really do some discovery to finally and make the choice to forgive. This includes the people who gave me most grief: my mother, my father, my situations, myself, the people who abused me and treated me like I was nothing.

Do you really want your life back and restored? Forgiveness is not just to grant others, but it is really and truthfully for you. Yes you! In order to move forward in life, you must release the other person from that guilt and resentment you held over their head. By doing this reconciling, you are able to set yourself free. Note forgiveness is not where you say "I forgive you," and you bring up the offense again using that as ammo against the person when you should have already squashed it and moved on. Forgiving someone sets you free from the anger, and a prison of resentment and pride. I like how Marianne Williamson says that "Forgiveness is not always easy. At times, it feels more painful than the wound we suffered, to forgive the one that inflicted it. And yet, there is no peace without forgiveness." Forgiveness is when you treat them as if nothing ever happened. Yes, the reality is that something did happen and you probably won't forget it, but it must not operate in your feelings and emotions. What helps me is to treat everyone, even the ones with which I am angry, with great respect. Okay you might say is that being fake? I have to keep it real right? You are being real and you don't want to be a bitter person your whole life. If I were upset at everything and everyone, I wouldn't have a job, wife, friends or family. So what's wrong with being nice? With letting go? It's that simple really. I discipline myself to think differently, adjust my attitude, and change my perception when something happens to me. I deserve to be happy. Don't you deserve to be happy and full of joy? It takes entirely too much energy to be negative and angry all the time. You have the power and control how you respond; don't just react, but respond in a respectable, assertive manner. Give the offense grace and mercy and you will receive the same to you in return. Stop beating yourself up every day, all day. Relax and take your time. Forgiveness is a day-to-day process, and the best medicine is time. Giving yourself time to heal and understand what forgiveness is and releasing angry roots is just the beginning of the forgiveness process. I did this for years due to the fact that I'm a very strong-minded person, and very critical on myself. At this moment you are young and what I suggest is you start right now. Please don't waste Life and energy on these things. That is why I am showing you and telling you now, so you can learn from my mistakes. What I want to do is challenge you right now to text, email or call someone that you may need to forgive or ask for forgiveness. Like me, you could be secretly angry and maybe you are punishing yourself behind the scenes for something you did wrong. Let yourself off the hook and forgive yourself. It was a mistake. Maybe you didn't mean to. Maybe it was an accident. I hope that as you have read this book, I have reached the concrete walls of your heart, to let you know it's safe again to open.

This is one of the most crucial chapters in this book. Forgiveness is a key component in combating anger and it can help you move past the hurt a little easier with an open heart and willingness to act upon it.

In your own words describe what forgiveness means to you?

_____
_____
_____
_____
_____
_____

What keeps you from forgiving yourself or others?

_____
_____
_____
_____
_____
_____
_____
_____

What would you like to see changed?

_____
_____
_____
_____
_____
_____
_____

(forgiveness is when you treat them as if it never happened.)

I'm not asking you to forgive and forget it's not easy. What I will ask you is if you feel you are able to treat the person/s or yourself as if the offense has never happened?

_____
_____
_____
_____
_____
_____
_____
_____
_____
_____
_____
_____
_____
_____

FREEDOM

As we come to a close I hope you saw and felt how anger has affected my life positively and negatively. You saw my anger and why I loved anger so much. I worshipped it and in my world, I became god of anger. It was all I ever really knew to do to cope with my emotions. This was my life! I lived this! I breathed this! I loved it! It was a false sense of being loved and idolizing an emotion to fill that hole in my life. Yes, I still had doubt and questions. Who am I? What am I doing here? And why me? Why am I so angry? When I understood what anger meant and watched how I operated in this strong emotion, I was able to answer these questions. To dig deep into those angry roots and have faith to uproot everything that had been a hindrance in being what I was created and designed to be was very difficult. Remember, it takes patience and consistency to accomplish anything challenging in life whether it be a diploma, degree or a life change. You are personally responsible for yourself and how you respond to anger. You have control over your thoughts. Become an expert in mastering your mind and become disciplined. Oh yeah, it's hard and you will "fail," but each failure is an attempt to practice perseverance, to challenge yourself even more. Don't worry, it's worth it. You may not feel like you're valuable to the world, but you are. Do this for yourself because you and your family deserve better. Don't disqualify yourself like I did by giving into extravagant self-pity parties. Don't believe the lies that nobody cares, nobody loves you, your father wasn't there or your mother was a drug addictcrack head. Speak life into the atmosphere. Life and death is in the power of the tongue; I choose life! Faith comes by hearing, so there will be a time when you speaking positively to yourself, it may be the only inspiration you will ever get sometimes.

I know you have dreams and a vision, whether it's for you or your family. Do you think you were born just to be an angry, mean, unsatisfied person in this life? No, he created to with the tools to heal patterns that limit your potential. Let's not live and dwell in our past; let's look forward to the future.

My journey to becoming free and healed has been rough, but I wanted to know the truth. I wanted to seek out the truth, other than the appearance of truth I made in my dysfunctional world. I used my personal system as a lifestyle or a way of life because I could easily tell someone off or act a fool if I didn't have my flesh under control. Here's some encouragement to look forward to. Since then, I have experienced great peace in my life. Peace and peace of mind is so important to me that you have no idea. I didn't know what that really was until I experienced it. You will appreciate every minute, especially if you have always had a dramatic lifestyle. Like I shared with you earlier, my wife and I started a non-profit organization called "The Man In Me." This consists of "Woman In Me" for our ladies, our youth, and specializing on our men and fathers. I forgave my mother for all the hell she put us through. This took years and years of practice, repetition, consistent and changing how I think daily. To be real with you, to be where I'm at right now, it took hard work. Back in the day, I went years without speaking to her or seeing her. I would curse her out and one time, I almost knocked her out. Yes, I know it's not cool and you are probably would not dare to think anything like this towards your mother, but that wasn't my mom. She was pure evil in my eyes. Since then, I have sat down with my father and had a real conversation about my life growing up. He filled in so many gaps in my life story that I never knew. I had been angry for so many years. I have been holding grudges against my father for nothing. He explained to me his story about how it all went down with my mother, my brothers and me. I expressed my thoughts, my feelings and how my life was, he kind of knew but never asked. I told him the truth and that growing up with my mother was pure hell. It was like living with the devil himself. I told him that our house was like the drug houses on TV where people lived doped out. Our house was exactly that, only with us being there and experiencing that every day. Although I understand that the drug addiction that was controlling her. No matter how much damage she had done, I know she loved me. I now choose life over death and choose to love her over anger. I would not have been born, or be the man I am today if it wasn't for my parents. My pain has brought me to my purpose.

I hungered for answers on how to forgive those who abused me and hurt me. (Again this is what worked for me and may not work for you.) I remember the most memorable and life changing event in forgiveness. It was at a event and the speaker asked if anyone had been abused in anyway please come up. All who went up were women. I went and as I sat there, I felt a tugging on my heart. I was too embarrassed because I didn't want people to think that I was a weak punk now. I said to myself, but "I need this…" All I know is that I walked up there and stood. Shortly after, I saw other men follow after me. I can't explain it. It was an intense night of something breaking in the spirit realm. They handed out pieces of paper and a pen to everyone. He asked us to write down who physically abused you, mentally abused you or abused you in any kind of way. I wrote my list down. As everyone was finished, he said "I want you to tear the paper up." He said that, "when you tear it up, you are breaking the power connected to that person, and you are to forgive them. So, when you tear it up, leave it on the floor and walk away." It's done! Can you imagine anything like this? It was a powerful night in my healing process.

You may think that all we did was write names and tear up a piece of paper, right? I'm sorry to let you know this was so much more that. I can't even describe in words. By physically tearing it up and letting the pieces fall to the ground, it did something inside of me. I felt a release from something. It felt like a heavy weight that was on me had been lifted because I was significantly lighter. It's time for you to let go of every hurt, every pain, every abusive encounter or bad relationship with others or self. So I am asking that you get a piece of paper and write a list of people who have offended you, abused you or hurt you in any kind of way that you haven't let go inside your heart. As you write down this down, I want you to look at the people on that list. Stare at it if you will, and remember it. If you're not ready just yet, that's okay. I want you to know that you already came this far in your journey to freedom in your life, why stop now? What's real is that you want your peace back, your hope back, your joy back, and your mind back. When you tear this list into pieces and walk away, you are leaving it at all at the altar as I did that night.

I want you to tear it up right now! Tear it up! By tearing the list you are signifying that you are releasing yourself from the pain, the hurt, the heartache, the abuse, the anger and the guilt. You are forgiving them for hurting you. This heavy luggage you have been carrying has been stopping you from being everything you are created to be. You need to do as I did and fight! Fight for your freedom! The chains of your past have been broken, ladies and gentlemen! (This approach may not work for everyone but it worked for me, give it a try you have nothing to lose.)

I hope this has been helpful to you on how to manage and use your anger in life. It's only the beginning! Congratulations, you're free at last! Live!

I am asking that you get a piece of paper and write a list of people who have offended you, abused you or hurt you in any kind of way that you haven't let go inside your heart. As you write down this down, I want you to look at the people on that list. Stare at it if you will, and remember it. If you're not ready just yet, that's okay. I want you to know that you already came this far in your journey to freedom in your life, why stop now?

Exercise: Writing the name of person/s you are forgiving.

1. _____
2. _____
3. _____
4. _____
5. _____
6. _____
7. _____
8. _____
9. _____
10. _____
11. _____
12. _____
13. _____
14. _____
15. _____
16. _____
17. _____
18. _____
19. _____
20. _____

When you tear this list into pieces and walk away, you are leaving it at all on the ground as I did that night.

I want you to tear it up right now! Tear it up! By tearing the list you are signifying that you are releasing yourself from the pain, the hurt, the heartache, the abuse, the anger and the guilt. You are forgiving them for hurting you. This heavy luggage you have been carrying has been stopping you from being everything you are created to be. You need to do as I did and fight! Fight for your freedom! The chains of your past have been broken, ladies and gentlemen! *(This approach may not work for everyone but it worked for me, give it a try you have nothing to lose.)*

REFLECTION

This can be a very misinterpreted subject, but I wanted to give you a different perspective and a new outlook in this emotion of anger. I hope you can get a taste of why I love anger. The real truth is because anger actually helped me to help you. I used that fight, that passion, and that energy, redirected that anger towards my destiny and purpose in my life. I transformed my selfish and prideful emotion into selfless action. I wished I had known my self-worth back then when I was doing mean things to people. A mindset would be like, "you or nobody is not going to disrespect what is valuable and sacred to me."

It motivated me to create change in my environment. This is real life for me. I saw that I needed to act quickly and change myself. I refused to continue being a victim, feeling ignorant and sorry for myself. I had enough already! I refused to pretend to be anyone else. When are you going to BE YOU? For me, I refused to be mediocre and do what others think I should do. I had to dig deep to decide what I really wanted out of life. Johann Wolfgang von Goethe said that, "I have come to the frightening conclusion that I am the decisive element. It is my personal approach that creates the climate. It is my daily mood that makes the weather. I possess tremendous power to make life miserable or joyous. I can be a tool of torture or an instrument of inspiration, I can humiliate or humor, hurt or heal. In all situations, it is my response that decides whether a crisis is escalated or de-escalated, and a person is humanized or de-humanized. If we treat people as they are, we make them worse. If we treat people as they ought to be, we help them become what they are capable of becoming." Do you want to destroy everything around you or build those things around you that will make a difference? Do you want to leave this world knowing that you made an impact and left a positive mark on this earth? Do you want to laugh, have fun, enjoy life, help others and, let's not forget, make some money?

I didn't want to die full of gifts, talents, visions and dreams that I never was able to experience. I deserve so much more! I am worth it! I am the greatest of all time! I am valuable and, yes, you are too! Don't let anyone tell you anything different! Do you hear me? Do you want to really experience more? I had to check myself and decide, if I didn't discover and tap into the "person in you" now, I would never find out who I really was and live out my mission in the universe.

I heard someone say one time that "the richest place in the world is the graveyard." Those gifts, talents, the love you have stopped giving to friends or family, visions, dreams and goals die with you. Wow! Huh!? Yes, but I'm here with you to help you see you, to find you, to live free, to live full and to die with your fuel tank on E!

Like I said earlier, the non-profit organization was birthed out of pain and anger. It was squeezed from the pain, the abuse, the rejection, the resentment, and the sacrifice of my childhood. Anger would have killed me if I allowed it to fully operate. Based on past hurts, rejection and the need to be accepted, I created a whole false world to protect myself from everything. I realized that the real enemy wasn't anyone else, it was me. I would have destroyed my life if had kept that negative and explosive anger inside of me. If I were to continue my behavior and operating out of my innermost thoughts and feelings, I would have killed myself. However, that anger actually gave life and a purpose because I didn't want to think negative any longer. I didn't want to be addicted to drama and anger. I didn't want to be the god of anger anymore. I just wanted to be Isaac. Sounds simple, huh? It's crazy when you imagine being you. My perspective had to change in order to change my life. When I saw myself in the mirror, looking at the "Person in Me" disappointed me. I was angry for what I had become because of the angry roots I didn't know how to deal with. Have you looked at yourself lately? I'm standing here looking at myself, as if I were a complete stranger. I said "I don't even know who you are? Who are you? Is this the true Isaac Rowe?" I was completely lost to what was happening in my life and what was real. The tool that was used against me, I used to help myself. The very thing that almost took me out brought me up. That very weapon the enemy used to fight against me, I used to fight for myself. The very thing I was allowing to destroy my life saved me and gave me hope. Anger is my fuel, my passion, my energy, my fight, my motivation and my inspiration.

My life now is blessed. I don't carry my old luggage with me like I used to. I carry the life lessons and experience over the years to share with others. I take responsibility for myself and my actions. I read inspiring books and develop myself daily. I focus on walking in love, patience, gentleness and peace. I want you to expect there will be challenges and it will not be easy. Take it one day at a time. You and I will fall short sometimes, but we need to push through anyway. It is a part of the growth process and undergoing a life changing experience.

Do you want to destroy everything around you or build up everything around you? Will it make a difference and why?

_____

_____

_____

_____

_____

_____

_____

_____

Do you want to leave this world knowing that you made an impact and left a positive mark on this earth? Why?

_____

_____

_____

_____

_____

_____

_____

_____

Do you remember in the beginning we talked about your dreams and goals? How do you feel about them now?

_____

_____

_____

_____

_____

Do you think you can use and direct your anger in a positive direction? How?

_____

_____

_____

_____

_____

_____

_____

_____

_____

What do you plan to do now? What will you do differently?

_____

_____

_____

_____

_____

_____

_____

_____

_____

_____

_____

_____

_____

_____

_____

I want you to expect there will be challenges and it will not be easy. Take it one day at a time. You and I will fall short sometimes, but we need to push through anyway. It is a part of the growth process and undergoing a life changing experience

ANGER GAME PLAN:

Let's specify positive **S.M.A.R.T.** goals. SMART goals are **S**pecific, **M**easureable, **A**chievable, **R**ealistic and **T**ime Framed.

Specific: Your goals should be realistic and address the "Angry Roots".

Measurable: You need to know how you will determine if you have reached your goal.

Achievable: Is this something you can really accomplish?

Realistic: Is this a goal you are fully committed and prepared to do?

Time Framed: How long will it take to or duration of time to reach this goal?

Write down 2 goals you would like to accomplish in 30 days. Write 2 goals you would like to accomplish in 6 months.

Over the next month, I want you to focus and track your progress using the example.

EXAMPLE:

Date: 01/01/2022

Goal: to communicate my feelings using "I" statements whenever I get angry at school or home.

Action Steps: I will track my daily progress on how many times I use "I" statements and my feelings in my journal.

Time frame: 01/01/2022 - 01/30/2022 = 30 days

Outcomes: 10 times out of the month I used "I" Statements. 8 times I was angry and disappointed. 2 times I was frustrated.

Homework Assignments:

1. Search on the Internet "I" Statements and learn about how to effectively communicate assertively.

2. Seach on the internet Anger Management Relaxation techniques and to use them. I will give you one.."Always remember to BREATHE"

POST ANGER SURVEY

Please answer the following questions as accurately and complete as possible.

1. How many times do you get angry NOW? (Check one that applies)
[ ] less than 5 times a day
[ ] more than 5 times a day.
[ ] several times a week.
[ ] a few times a month.
[ ] rarely.

2. NOW, I get angry when? (Check all that apply)
[ ] My friends are being bullied verbally, emotionally or physically.
[ ] I am treated unfairly.
[ ] Feel depressed.
[ ] Name-calling or teasing/bullied
[ ] People will not listen to me. (Friends, Parents, Teachers, Other_____)
[ ] Someone tries to take something from me
[ ] People don't give me a chance.
[ ] People reject me or don't accept me
[ ] I am not loved by family
[ ] I'm not able to voice my opinion
[ ] Someone damages my property
[ ] Anyone pushes or hits me, or someone close to me
[ ] People don't understand my feelings
[ ] People don't have time for me.
[ ] I feel like I don't matter.
[ ] People tell me what to do
[ ] Losing a game or a contest
[ ] Mistreatment of animals

3. NOW, When I get angry I? (Check all that apply)
[ ] Hit someone or something.
[ ] Hurt myself
[ ] Throw things
[ ] I tell a friend teacher or parent.
[ ] Keep it inside
[ ] I raise my voice and get really loud
[ ] Become cynical or sarcastic.
[ ] Relax and Breathe
[ ] Use anger management tools
[ ] Think about how I can get even.
[ ] Smile and play it off as a joke.
[ ] I argue and curse at people
[ ] Blackout
Other _____

POSITIVE AFFIRMTIONS

My name is_____
I am in control.
I am good.
I am confident.
I am competent.
I am worthy of success.
I am a gifted human being.
I am blessed.
I am respected.
I am admired.
I am valuable.
I am loved.
I am a kind and loving person.
I am what I say I am, not others.
I contribute to the world.
I am a finisher.
I can deal with conflict.
I can handle anger.
I can deal with stress.
I will be the best ME I can be.

Add to the list of your own positive affirmations

_____
_____
_____
_____
_____
_____
_____
_____
_____
_____
_____
_____
_____

FEEDBACK

Did you learn more about yourself ? (Circle)   Yes   No   Somewhat

(Explain why your answer)

_____

_____

_____

_____

What tools did you get out of this book/class? (Explain)

_____

_____

_____

Write down one word that you would describe this book/class?

_____

If you could go back in time what would you say to yourself NOW after you understand more about anger?

_____

_____

_____

_____

What advice would you give other youth like you?

_____

_____

_____

CPSIA information can be obtained
at www.ICGtesting.com
Printed in the USA
LVHW062321310119
606046LV00007B/127/P